Welcome Home

8 Inviting Wall Hangings

Welcome Home: 8 Inviting Wall Hangings
© 2015 by Martingale & Company®

Martingale
19021 120th Ave. NE, Ste. 102
Bothell, WA 98011-9511 USA
ShopMartingale.com

Printed in China
20 19 18 17 16 15   8 7 6 5 4 3 2 1

Library of Congress Cataloging-in-Publication Data is available upon request.
ISBN: 978-1-60468-577-0

Mission Statement
Dedicated to providing quality products
and service to inspire creativity.

Projects in this book have previously been published in:
Pretty Patchwork Quilts by Cyndi Walker; *Fast and Fun First Quilts* by Sara Dipersloot; *Nine by Nine* by Cyndi Hershey; *Folk-Art Favorites* by Avis Shier and Tammy Johnson; *Quilting for Joy* by Barbara Brandeburg and Teri Christopherson; *Bloom Creek Quilts* by Vicki Bellino; and *The Blue and the Gray* by Mary Etherington and Connie Tesene.

What's your creative passion?
Find it at **ShopMartingale.com**
books • eBooks • ePatterns • daily blog • free projects
videos • tutorials • inspiration • giveaways

Contents

Honey Bee

Take just a dash of patchwork, add a pinch of appliqué for the Honey Bee blocks, and you'll have a quilt that's both a delight to make and sweet to behold.

Designed and pieced by Cyndi Walker; quilted by Pamela Dransfeldt

Quilt size: 44½" x 44½" • **Block size:** 16" x 16"

Materials

Yardage is based on 42"-wide fabric.

1⅓ yards total of assorted blue, peach, green, and yellow prints for blocks and pieced outer border

⅝ yard of cream tone on tone for blocks

⅜ yard of peach solid for inner border

⅜ yard of peach print for appliquéd teardrops

⅓ yard of yellow tone on tone for blocks

⅜ yard of peach floral for binding

3 yards of fabric for backing

54" x 54" piece of batting

Clear monofilament or matching embroidery thread for machine appliqué

Water-soluble fabric glue

Template plastic or freezer paper

Cutting

Measurements include ¼"-wide seam allowances.

From the assorted blue, peach, green, and yellow prints, cut *a total of:*
16 strips, 2½" x 42"

From the cream tone on tone, cut:
4 strips, 4½" x 42"; crosscut into 16 rectangles, 4½" x 8½"

From the yellow tone on tone, cut:
2 strips, 4½" x 42"; crosscut into 16 squares, 4½" x 4½"

From the peach solid, cut:
2 strips, 2½" x 36½"
2 strips, 2½" x 32½"

From the peach floral, cut:
5 strips, 2¼" x 42"

Making the Blocks

1 Selecting different colors, sew together four assorted blue, peach, green, and yellow 2½" x 42" strips along the long edges to make a strip set. Repeat this process for the remaining assorted strips to make a total of four strip sets. Cut each strip set into 14 segments, 2½" wide, for a total of 56 segments.

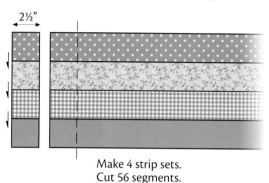

2½"

Make 4 strip sets.
Cut 56 segments.

2 Arrange four different strip-set segments into rows and sew together; press the seam allowances in either direction. Make four units. The remaining strip-set segments will be used later in the pieced border.

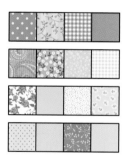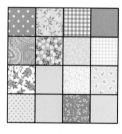

Make 4.

3 Arrange the block center, four cream 4½" x 8½" rectangles, and four yellow 4½" squares as shown. Sew the pieces into rows; press the seam allowances as shown. Sew the rows together to form the pieced block; press the seam allowances away from the block center. Make four blocks.

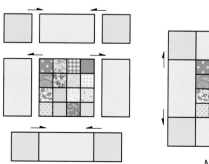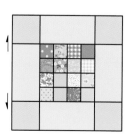

Make 4.

Appliquéing the Blocks

1 Using the peach print and the patterns on page 7, prepare 16 large teardrops and 32 small teardrops for your favorite method of appliqué. The quilt shown was made using the invisible machine-appliqué technique. For this technique, cut freezer-paper pattern pieces. Iron the freezer paper onto the wrong side of the appliqué fabric and cut the shapes from the fabric, adding a ¼" seam allowance. Press the seam allowances to the wrong side using the freezer-paper edge as a guide. Remove the paper and press again to ensure the seam allowances stay in place.

2 Referring to the appliqué placement diagram below, position four large teardrops and eight small teardrops onto a pieced block. Cyndi glue-basted her appliqués in place.

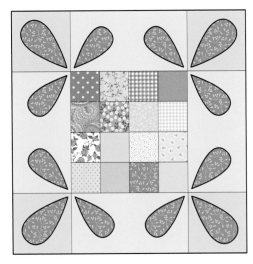

Appliqué placement

3 Using clear monofilament or coordinating thread, stitch the appliqué pieces in place. Repeat the appliqué process for each of the remaining three blocks.

Assembling the Quilt Top

1 Referring to the quilt assembly diagram on page 7, arrange four appliquéd blocks into two rows of two blocks each. Sew the blocks together in rows; press in opposite directions. Sew the rows together to make the quilt center.

2 Sew the peach-solid 2½" x 32½" strips to the left and right edges of the quilt center; press the seam allowances toward the border. Sew the peach-solid 2½" x 36½" strips to the top and bottom edges of the quilt center; press the seam allowances toward the border.

3 Using the leftover strip-set segments, sew 32 segments together in pairs to make 16 units for the border strips. Separate eight segments into two units each and make eight four-patch units. Sew the pairs and four-patch units into rows as shown; make two of each.

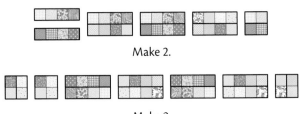

Make 2.

Make 2.

4 Sew the shorter pieced border strips to the left and right edges of the quilt; press the seam allowances toward the pieced border. Sew the remaining pieced border strips to the top and bottom edges of the quilt; press the seam allowances toward the pieced border.

Finishing the Quilt

For more information on finishing techniques, go to ShopMartingale.com/HowtoQuilt for free illustrated instructions.

1 Prepare the quilt backing.

2 Layer the quilt top, batting, and backing; baste the layers together.

3 Hand or machine quilt as desired.

4 Trim the backing and batting even with the quilt top, and then use the peach-floral 2¼"-wide strips to finish the edges of your quilt. Add a label and sleeve if desired.

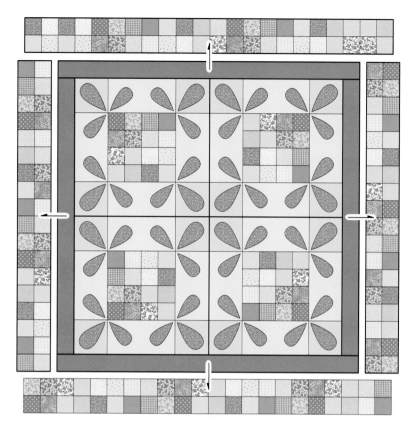

Quilt assembly

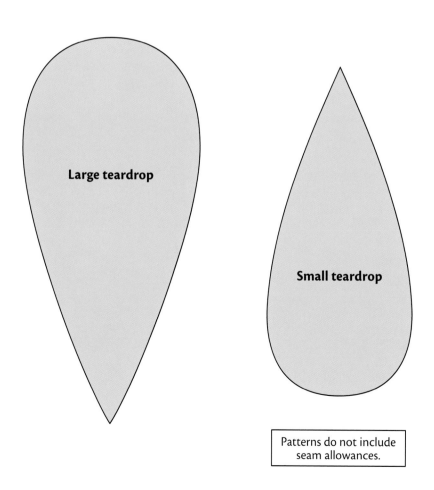

Large teardrop

Small teardrop

Patterns do not include
seam allowances.

Tilted Spools

The Spool block is a traditional favorite among quiltmakers.
Cyndi challenges you to dive into your stash for this scrappy—
and easy—spin on the Spool block.

Designed by Cyndi Walker; pieced by Debbie Gray; quilted by Pamela Dransfeldt

Quilt size: 48½" x 64½" • **Block size:** 8" x 8"

Materials

Yardage is based on 42"-wide fabric.

2⅝ yards total of assorted cream prints for blocks
1⅜ yards total of assorted aqua, tan, pink, and green prints for blocks
½ yard of yellow print for binding
3¼ yards of fabric for backing
58" x 74" piece of batting

Cutting

Measurements include ¼"-wide seam allowances.

From the assorted cream prints, cut:
48 squares, 5" x 5"
48 *pairs* of squares, 4½" x 4½", to match the
    5" squares (96 total)

From the assorted aqua, tan, pink, and green prints, cut:
48 squares, 5" x 5"
48 *pairs* of matching squares, 2½" x 2½" (96 total)

From the yellow print, cut:
6 strips, 2¼" x 42"

Making the Blocks

For each block, choose one cream 5" square and two cream 4½" squares, all from the same print. Choose one print 5" square and two matching print 2½" squares that coordinate with the chosen print 5" square.

1 Draw a diagonal line from corner to corner on the wrong side of the cream 5" square. With right sides together, layer the print 5" square and the marked cream square; sew ¼" from each side of the drawn line. Cut along the drawn line to make two half-square-triangle units; press the seam allowances toward the print. Trim the units to 4½" x 4½".

2 Draw a diagonal line on the wrong side of the two matching print 2½" squares. Align a marked square with one corner of a cream 4½" square and sew along the marked line. Trim the excess fabric, leaving a ¼" seam allowance, and press the seam allowances toward the corner. Repeat to make two corner units.

Make 2.

3 Arrange the two half-square-triangle units and the two corner units as shown. Sew the units in each row together; press the seam allowances toward the half-square-triangle units. Sew the rows together to complete the block; press.

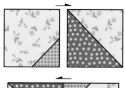

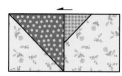

4 Repeat steps 1–3 to make a total of 48 blocks.

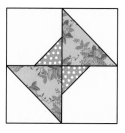

Make 48.

Assembling the Quilt Top

Referring to the quilt assembly diagram below, arrange the blocks into eight rows of six blocks each, alternating the angle of the spools from block to block. Sew the blocks in each row together, pressing the seam allowances in opposite directions from row to row. Sew the rows together and press all seam allowances in one direction to complete the quilt top.

Finishing the Quilt

For more information on finishing techniques, go to ShopMartingale.com/HowtoQuilt for free illustrated instructions.

1 Prepare the quilt backing.

2 Layer the quilt top, batting, and backing; baste the layers together.

3 Hand or machine quilt as desired.

4 Trim the backing and batting even with the quilt top, and then use the yellow 2¼"-wide strips to finish the edges of your quilt. Add a label and sleeve if desired.

Quilt assembly

Harvest Star

Whether you're having a leaf-raking party or celebrating Thanksgiving, this triple-star quilt makes the perfect backdrop for all things fall. Hang it on the wall, or drape its spicy, warm autumnal colors on your table.

Designed and pieced by Sara Diepersloot; quilted by Deborah Rasmussen

Quilt size: 47" x 47"

Materials

Yardage is based on 42"-wide fabric.

⅞ yard of gold leaf print for blocks

¾ yard of tan leaf print for border 4

⅝ yard of large-scale pumpkin print for blocks

⅝ yard of brown plaid for border 2 and binding

⅓ yard of rust print #1 for blocks

⅓ yard of rust print #2 for border 1

¼ yard of small-scale pumpkin print for blocks

¼ yard of gold star print for border 3

⅛ yard of brown pumpkin print for blocks

⅛ yard of gold dot for blocks

1 fat eighth or 5" x 5" piece of pumpkin plaid for center square

3⅛ yards of fabric for backing

55" x 55" piece of batting

Cutting

Measurements include ¼"-wide seam allowances.

From the gold dot, cut:
1 strip, 2½" x 42"; crosscut into 8 squares, 2½" x 2½"

From the brown pumpkin print, cut:
1 strip, 2½" x 42"; crosscut into:
    4 rectangles, 2½" x 4½"
    4 squares, 2½" x 2½"

From the pumpkin plaid, cut:
1 square, 4½" x 4½"

From the small-scale pumpkin print, cut:
1 strip, 4½" x 42"; crosscut into 8 squares, 4½" x 4½"

From rust print #1, cut:
2 strips, 4½" x 42"; crosscut into:
    4 rectangles, 4½" x 8½"
    4 squares, 4½" x 4½"

From the large-scale pumpkin print, cut:
2 strips, 8½" x 42"; crosscut into 8 squares, 8½" x 8½"

From the gold leaf print, cut:
3 strips, 8½" x 42"; crosscut into:
    4 rectangles, 8½" x 16½"
    4 squares, 8½" x 8½"

From rust print #2, cut:
4 strips, 2" x 42"

From the brown plaid, cut:
4 strips, 1½" x 42"
5 strips, 2¼" x 42"

From the gold star print, cut:
4 strips, 1¼" x 42"

From the tan leaf print, cut:
5 strips, 4½" x 42"

Making the Blocks

Press all seam allowances as indicated by the arrows in the diagrams.

1 Draw a diagonal line from corner to corner on the wrong side of the gold-dot 2½" squares.

2 Lay a marked square on one end of a brown-pumpkin 2½" x 4½" rectangle, right sides together. Sew on the drawn line. Trim off the excess ¼" from the stitching line. Press the seam allowances toward the triangle. Repeat on the other end of the rectangle, orienting the diagonal line in the opposite direction. Make four of these star-point units.

Make 4.

3 Arrange the brown-pumpkin 2½" squares, the star-point units, and the pumpkin-plaid 4½" square as shown. Join the units into rows, and then sew the rows together. Press.

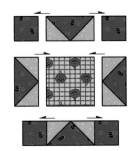 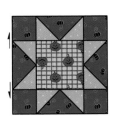

4 Draw a diagonal line from corner to corner on the wrong side of the small-scale pumpkin-print 4½" squares. Repeat step 2, placing the squares on a rust-print 4½" x 8½" rectangle. Make four of these star-point units.

 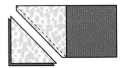

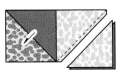 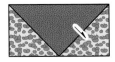

Make 4.

5 Arrange the rust 4½" squares, the star-point units from step 4, and the star unit made in step 3 as shown. Join the units into rows, and then sew the rows together. Press.

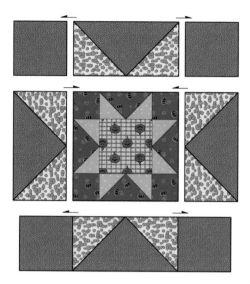

6 Draw a diagonal line from corner to corner on the wrong side of the large-scale pumpkin-print 8½" squares. Repeat step 2, placing the squares on a gold leaf-print 8½" x 16½" rectangle. Make four of these star-point units.

7 Arrange the gold leaf-print 8½" squares, the star-point units from step 4, and the star unit made in step 5 as shown. Join the units into rows, and then sew the rows together. Press.

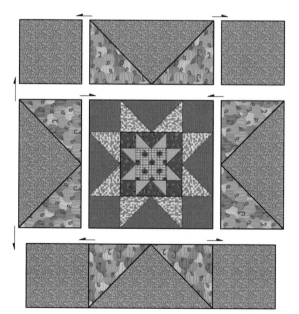

Assembling the Quilt Top

Measure the length of the quilt top first, and then trim two of the rust border strips to that length and joint them to the sides of the quilt top. Press the seam allowances toward the border strips. Measure the width of the quilt top and trim the remaining rust border strips to that length. Sew them to the top and bottom of the quilt top; press. Repeat the process of measuring and adding borders to fit, adding them in this order: rust print, brown plaid, gold star print, and tan leaf print. Press after each addition.

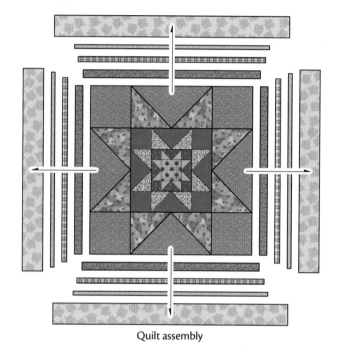

Quilt assembly

Finishing the Quilt

For more information on finishing techniques, go to ShopMartingale.com/HowtoQuilt for free illustrated instructions.

1 Prepare the quilt backing.

2 Layer the quilt top, batting, and backing; baste the layers together.

3 Hand or machine quilt as desired.

4 Trim the backing and batting even with the quilt top, and then use the brown-plaid 2¼"-wide strips to finish the edges of your quilt. Add a label and sleeve if desired.

Diamonz

An elongated block featuring strong diagonal lines creates a design that keeps your eyes moving. Select fabrics with minimal pattern for the blocks, such as the tonal batiks used here, to help increase the overall visual impact.

Designed and pieced by Cyndi Hershey; quilted by Pat Burns

Quilt size: 48½" x 66½" • **Block size:** 6" x 9"

Materials

Yardage is based on 42"-wide fabric.

3½ yards of dark-pink batik for blocks, outer border, and binding

1⅞ yards of light-pink batik for blocks

⅓ yard of yellow batik for inner border

3¼ yards of fabric for backing

54" x 72" piece of batting

Cutting

Measurements include ¼"-wide seam allowances.

From the dark-pink batik, cut:

23 strips, 2½" x 42"; crosscut 10 strips into 108 rectangles, 2½" x 3½"

From the *remainder* of the dark pink batik, cut on the *lengthwise grain*:

2 strips, 5½" x 56½"

2 strips, 5½" x 48½"

From the light-pink batik, cut:

24 strips, 2½" x 42"; crosscut 17 strips into 180 rectangles, 2½" x 3½"

From the yellow batik, cut:

5 strips, 1½" x 42"

Making the Blocks

1 Draw a diagonal line from the top-right corner to the bottom-left corner on the wrong side of 54 light-pink rectangles. On the remaining 54 light-pink rectangles, draw the diagonal line in the opposite direction.

Make 54.   Make 54.

2 With right sides together, place a marked light rectangle diagonally on top of a dark-pink rectangle with the drawn line of the top rectangle connecting the intersecting corners of the bottom rectangle as shown above right. Sew on the drawn line. Cut ¼" away from the drawn line. Press the seam allowances toward the dark print. Repeat to make 54 half-rectangle units and 54 mirror-image units; 108 total.

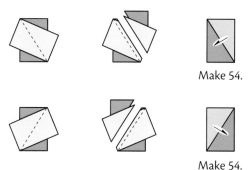

Make 54.

Make 54.

3 Sew dark and light 2½" x 42" strips together in pairs as shown to make seven strip sets. Press the seam allowances toward the light strips. Crosscut the strip sets into 72 segments, 3½" wide.

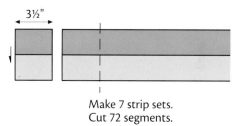

3½"

Make 7 strip sets.
Cut 72 segments.

4 Lay out three half-rectangle units, two strip-set segments, and two light 2½" x 3½" rectangles in three rows. Join the pieces in each row using *scant* ¼" seam allowances. Press the seam allowances toward the light rectangles in each row. Sew the rows together using a *slightly generous* ¼" seam allowance; see "Get the Point" on page 16. Press the seam allowances toward the outer rows. Repeat to make a total of 18 blocks of each type.

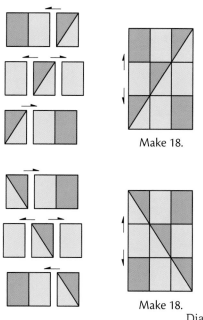

Make 18.

Make 18.

Get the Point

Because the unit shape is a rectangle and not a square, when two ¼" seams intersect at the corner, they don't meet exactly at the seam point. To compensate for this slight difference, sew the vertical seams in each row with a *scant* seam allowance and the horizontal seams that join the rows with a *generous* seam allowance. This method eliminates the need to use templates to cut the triangles for this quilt.

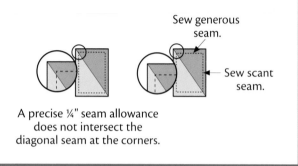

A precise ¼" seam allowance does not intersect the diagonal seam at the corners.

Assembling the Quilt Top

1 Refer to the quilt assembly diagram above right to lay out the blocks in six rows of six blocks each. Sew the blocks in each row together using a *scant* ¼" seam allowance. Press the seam allowances in opposite directions from row to row.

2 Sew the rows together using a *generous* ¼" seam allowance. Press all seam allowances in one direction.

3 Sew the yellow strips together end to end and press the seam allowances open. From the pieced strip, cut two 1½" x 54½" strips and two 1½" x 38½" strips. Sew the 1½" x 54½" strips to the sides of the quilt center. Press the seam allowances toward the yellow strips. Sew the 1½" x 38½" strips to the top and bottom of the quilt. Press the seam allowances toward the yellow strips.

4 Sew the dark-pink 5½" x 56½" strips to the sides of the quilt. Press the seam allowances toward the pink strips. Sew the dark-pink 5½" x 48½" strips to the top and bottom of the quilt. Press the seam allowances toward the dark-pink strips.

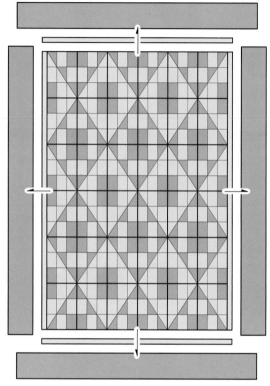

Quilt assembly

Finishing the Quilt

For more information on finishing techniques, go to ShopMartingale.com/HowtoQuilt for free illustrated instructions.

1 Prepare the quilt backing.

2 Layer the quilt top, batting, and backing; baste the layers together.

3 Hand or machine quilt as desired. The sample quilt features a large-scale puzzle design. This simple style of quilting allows for the overall design to be clearly visible without any distraction.

4 Trim the backing and batting even with the quilt top, and then use the remaining dark-pink 2½"-wide strips to finish the edges of your quilt. Add a label and sleeve if desired.

He Loves Me, He Loves Me Not

Gerbera daisies are bright and colorful. As you make this quilt, imagine how much fun it would be to pull off petals, one by one, deciding the fate of true love.

Designed and made by Avis Shirer; quilted by Sue Urich

Quilt size: 36" x 48" • **Block size:** 8" x 12"

Materials

Yardage is based on 42"-wide fabric.

⅓ yard each of pink, orange, yellow, red, and rose fabrics for flower appliqués

1 yard of red polka dot for outer border, sashing squares, and binding

⅞ yard of light print for appliqué block backgrounds

¼ yard each of pink print, green plaid, and taupe solid for pieced sashing and pieced inner border

⅓ yard of green print for bias stems and leaf appliqués

1⅔ yards of fabric for backing

42" x 54" piece of batting

1 yard of paper-backed fusible web

9 assorted buttons, 1⅜"-diameter

Cutting

Measurements include ¼"-wide seam allowances.

Use the appliqué patterns on page 20 to prepare flowers and leaves for fusible appliqué. For information on fusible appliqué, go to ShopMartingale.com/HowtoQuilt for free downloadable instructions.

From the light print, cut: *Background*

3 strips, 8½" x 42"; crosscut into 9 rectangles, 8½" x 12½"

From the green print, cut:

9 bias strips, 1" x 10"

12 leaves

From *each* of the pink, orange, yellow, and red fabrics, cut:

2 flowers (8 total)

From the rose fabric, cut:

1 flower

From the pink print, cut:

3 strips, 2½" x 42"; crosscut into:

24 squares, 2½" x 2½"

24 rectangles, 1½" x 2½"

From the taupe solid, cut:

3 strips, 2½" x 42"; crosscut into:

18 squares, 2½" x 2½"

24 rectangles, 1½" x 2½"

From the green plaid, cut:

3 strips, 2½" x 42"; crosscut into:

18 squares, 2½" x 2½"

22 rectangles, 1½" x 2½"

From the red polka dot, cut:

2 strips, 3½" x 30½"

3 strips, 3½" x 42"

4 squares, 2½" x 2½"

5 strips, 2½" x 42"

Making the Blocks

1 Press under ¼" along each long edge of the green 1" x 10" bias strips to make the stem pieces. Trim three of these pieces to 8" long.

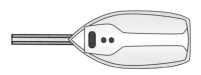

2 Position an 8" stem along the vertical center of three light-print rectangles, with the stem ends even with the bottom edges of the rectangles. The top ends will be covered by the flower appliqués. Appliqué the stems in place by hand or machine. Avis used a machine blind hem stitch. Appliqué the remaining stems to the remaining six light rectangles in the same manner, positioning three stems 1½" from the left side of the rectangles and three stems 1½" from the right side of the rectangles. Make a gentle curve in each of these stems that begins approximately 4½" from the bottom of the rectangle.

Make 3.

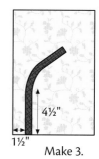
4½"
1½"
Make 3.

4½"
Make 3.
1½"

3 Peel the paper backing off of the prepared flower and leaf appliqués and place a flower over the top end of each stem. To create interest, rotate the flower shapes so that each block is slightly different

from the others. See the quilt photo on page 17 for ideas. When you're happy with the placement, fuse the shapes in place. Next, position the leaves on the stems: place one leaf on each of the six blocks with curved stems and two leaves on each of the three blocks with straight stems. When you're happy with the placement, fuse the leaves in place. Machine blanket-stitch around the flowers and leaves with matching thread.

Making the Sashing Strips

1 Sew together two pink 2½" squares, two taupe 2½" squares, and two green-plaid 2½" squares in the order shown. Repeat to make a total of six vertical sashing strips. Press all seam allowances in one direction.

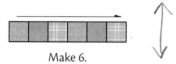

Make 6.

2 Sew together six pink 2½" squares, three green-plaid 2½" squares, three taupe 2½" squares, and two red polka-dot 2½" squares in the order shown. Repeat to make a total of two horizontal sashing strips. Press all seam allowances in one direction.

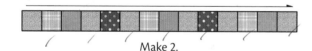

Make 2.

Assembling the Quilt Top

Press all seam allowances as indicated by the arrows in the assembly diagram.

1 Refer to the assembly diagram above right to arrange one of each block variation and two vertical sashing strips into a row. Sew the pieces together. Repeat to make a total of three rows. Join the rows, adding a horizontal sashing strip between each row.

2 For the inner borders, alternately stitch together the pink, taupe, and green-plaid 1½" x 2½" rectangles. Use 14 rectangles for each top and bottom border and 21 rectangles for each side border. Sew the top and bottom borders to the top and bottom of the quilt top. Sew the side borders to the sides of the quilt top.

3 For the outer borders, sew the red polka-dot 3½" x 30½" strips to the top and bottom of the quilt top. Sew the three red polka-dot 3½" x 42" strips together end to end. From the pieced strip, cut two strips, 3½" x 48½", and sew them to the sides of the quilt top.

Quilt assembly

Finishing the Quilt

For more information on finishing techniques, go to ShopMartingale.com/HowtoQuilt for free illustrated instructions.

1 Prepare the quilt backing.

2 Layer the quilt top, batting, and backing; baste the layers together.

3 Hand or machine quilt as desired. The quilt shown was machine quilted by echoing the flower and leaves in the blocks and with diamonds in each individual sashing square.

4 Trim the backing and batting even with the quilt top, and then use the red polka-dot 2½"-wide strips to finish the edges of your quilt. Add a label and sleeve if desired.

5 Sew a button to the center of each flower shape.

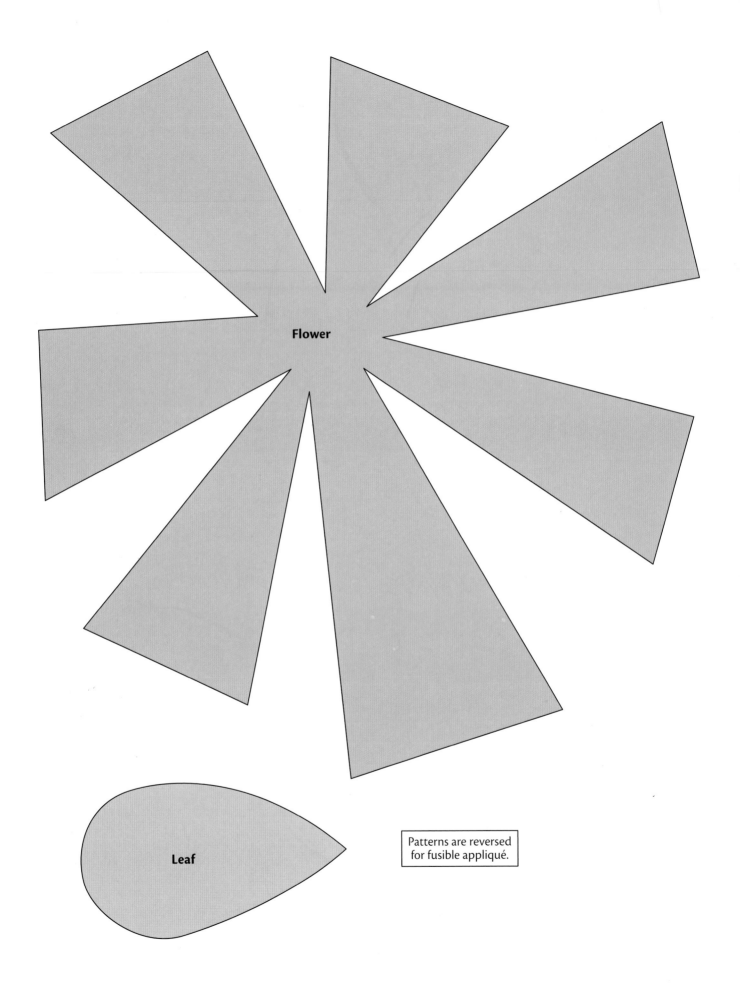

Flower

Leaf

Patterns are reversed
for fusible appliqué.

Wild Pears

After spending hours with her sister trying to peel apples, Barbara wondered why the apples all turned to mush. Too late, they realized they were actually peeling little green pears. This design is an ode to their wild pear night.

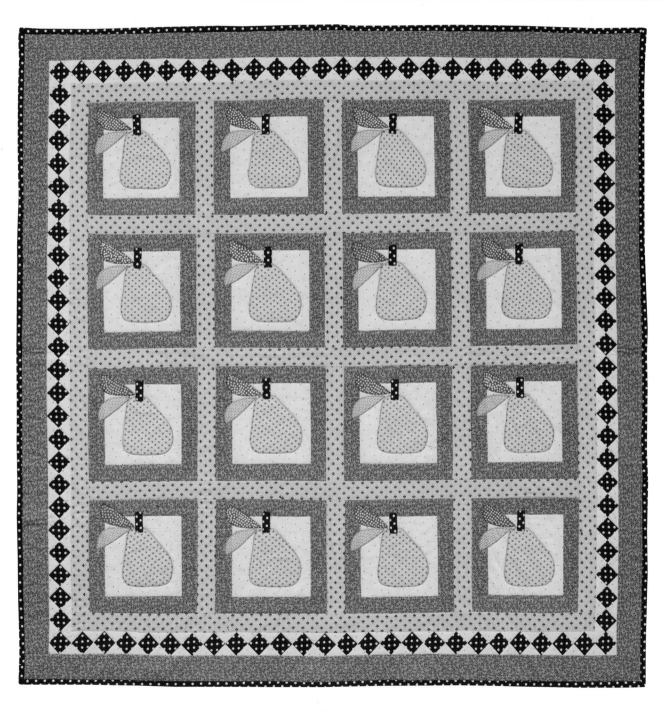

Designed and made by Barbara Brandenburg

Quilt size: 60" x 60" • **Block size:** 10½" x 10½"

Materials

Yardage is based on 42"-wide fabric.

1¾ yards of off-white print for block backgrounds and pieced border

1⅔ yards of blue print for blocks and outer border

1⅛ yards of brown print for stems, pieced border, and binding

1 yard of cream print for sashing and inner border

½ yard of yellow print for pears

⅛ yard *each* of 2 green prints for leaves

3⅞ yards of fabric for backing

66" x 66" piece of batting

1⅞ yards of fusible web

Cutting

Measurements include ¼"-wide seam allowances.

From the blue print, cut:
32 rectangles, 2" x 8"
32 rectangles, 2" x 11"
6 strips, 3" x 42"

From the off-white print, cut:
16 squares, 8" x 8"
10 strips, 2" x 42"
8 squares, 2" x 2"

From the cream print, cut:
12 rectangles, 2¼" x 11"
10 strips, 2¼" x 42"

From the brown print, cut:*
5 strips, 2" x 42"
7 strips, 2½" x 42"

*The remaining brown print will be used for stem appliqués.

Making the Blocks

For more information on fusible appliqué, go to ShopMartingale.com/HowtoQuilt for free downloadable instructions.

1 Sew blue 2" x 8" rectangles to two sides of an off-white 8" square. Press the seam allowances toward the blue. Sew the blue 2" x 11" rectangles to the top and bottom of the square. Press the seam allowances toward the blue. Repeat to make a total of 16 background squares.

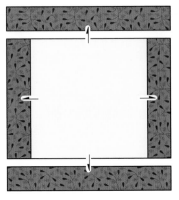

Make 16.

2 Using the patterns on page 25, prepare the pears, leaves, and stems for fusible appliqué. Make 16 pears from the yellow print, 16 stems from the remaining brown print, 16 of leaf A from one green fabric, and 16 of leaf B from the other green fabric.

3 Referring to the placement guide below, position the shapes on the background squares. Iron to fuse in place. Appliqué the edges of each shape using a narrow blanket stitch and brown thread.

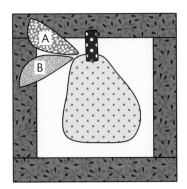

Appliqué placement

Assembling the Quilt Top

1 Alternately join four blocks and three cream 2¼" x 11" sashing strips. Repeat to make a total of four block rows. Press the seam allowances toward the sashing.

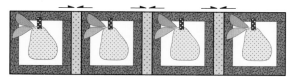

Make 4.

2 Sew the cream 2¼"-wide strips together end to end to make one long strip. From this strip, cut five sashing/border strips, 47¾" long, and two border strips, 51¼" long. Alternately join the block rows and 47¾"-long sashing strips. Press the seam allowances toward the sashing.

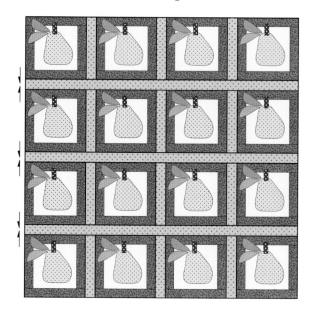

3 Sew the remaining 47¾"-long strips to the sides of the quilt, and then sew the 51¼"-long strips to the top and bottom of the quilt. Press the seam allowances toward the cream strips.

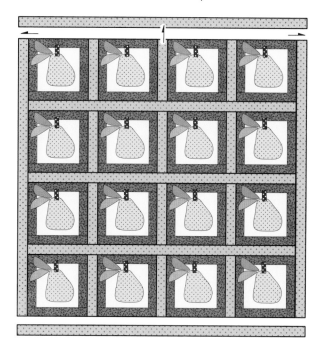

4 Sew one brown and two off-white 2"-wide strips together along the long edges to make a strip set. Repeat to make a total of five strip sets. Crosscut the strip sets into 100 segments, 2" wide. Press the seam allowances toward the brown strips.

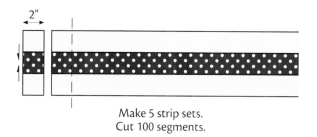

Make 5 strip sets.
Cut 100 segments.

5 Join 24 segments together as shown. Repeat to make a total of two pieced strips for the side borders. Sew an additional off-white 2" square to each end of the strips. Join 26 units in the same manner. Repeat to make a total of two pieced strips for the top and bottom borders. Sew an additional off-white 2" square to each end of the strips. Press the seam allowances open, pressing gently to avoid stretching the bias edges.

6 Trim the top, bottom, and ends of each pieced border ¼" outside the points of the brown squares. The long edges are on the bias and will stretch easily; handle them with care to keep the borders the proper size.

7 Sew the side pieced borders to the sides of the quilt, and then sew the top and bottom pieced borders to the top and bottom of the quilt. **Hint:** Sew with the pieced border on the bottom to keep it from stretching out of shape. Press the seam allowances toward the inner cream border.

8 Sew the blue 3"-wide strips together end to end to make one long piece. From this piece, cut two border strips, 55½" long, and two border strips, 60½"

long. Sew the 55½"-long strips to the sides of the quilt, and then sew the 60½"-long strips to the top and bottom of the quilt. Press the seam allowances toward the blue border.

Finishing the Quilt

For more information on finishing techniques, go to ShopMartingale.com/HowtoQuilt for free illustrated instructions.

1 Prepare the quilt backing.

2 Layer the quilt top, batting, and backing; baste the layers together.

3 Hand or machine quilt as desired.

4 Trim the backing and batting even with the quilt top, and then use the brown 2½"-wide strips to finish the edges of your quilt. Add a label and sleeve if desired.

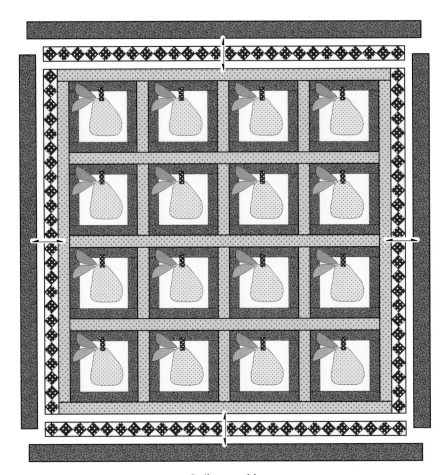

Quilt assembly

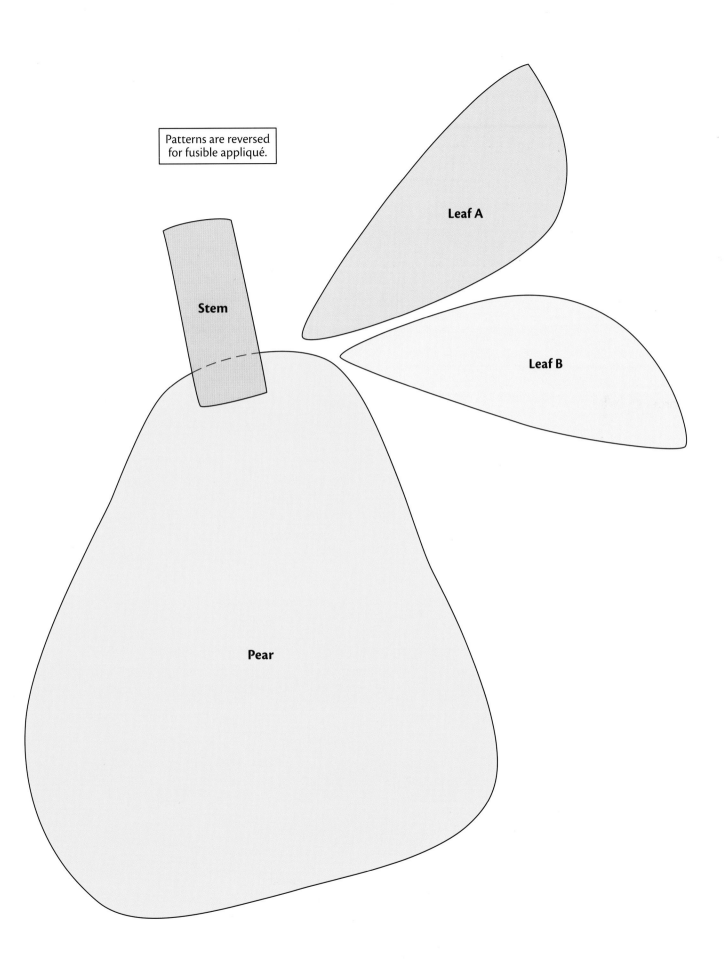

Patterns are reversed
for fusible appliqué.

Leaf A

Leaf B

Stem

Pear

"Oh" Americana

If you love all things Americana, this quilt is for you! The blocks are easy to piece whether starting with charm squares or fat quarters, and the stars and berries are simply fused in place.

Designed by Vicki Bellino; made by Susan Armington; quilted by Veronica Nurmi
Quilt size: 50" x 50" • **Block size:** 9" x 9"

Materials

Yardage is based on 42"-wide fabric. Fat quarters are approximately 18" x 21" and charm squares are 5" x 5".

4 fat quarters *each* of red and blue prints for blocks and appliqué*

1⅛ yards of small-scale cream print for outer border

⅞ yard of red print for inner border and binding

2 fat quarters *each* of cream and tan prints for blocks

½ yard of blue tone on tone for bias vine

3 yards of fabric for backing

54" x 54" piece of batting

1 yard of lightweight fusible web (12" wide)

½"-wide bias bar (optional)

For a scrappier look, substitute charm squares for the fat quarters. You'll need 32 red and 32 blue 5" squares.

Cutting

Measurements include ¼"-wide seam allowances.

Use the appliqué patterns on page 29 to prepare the stars and circles for fusible appliqué.

For more information on fusible appliqué, go to ShopMartingale.com/HowtoQuilt for free downloadable instructions.

From *each* of the red and blue fat quarters, cut:
8 squares, 5" x 5" (total of 32 red and 32 blue)

From the remainder of the red and blue fat quarters, cut:
2 large stars
6 medium stars
8 small stars
13 large circles
59 small circles

From *each* of the cream and tan fat quarters, cut:
16 squares, 3½" x 3½" (total of 32 cream and 32 tan)
16 squares, 2" x 2" (total of 32 cream and 32 tan)

From the red print, cut:
4 strips, 2½" x 42"
6 binding strips, 2" x 42"

From the blue tone on tone, cut:
1½"-wide bias strips to total 110" in length

From the small-scale cream print, cut:
5 strips, 5½" x 42"

Making the Blocks

1 Draw a diagonal line from corner to corner on the wrong side of each of the cream and tan 3½" and 2" squares.

2 With right sides together, place a tan 2" square on the upper-left corner of each blue 5" square. Sew on the drawn line, trim leaving a ¼" seam allowance, and press the seam allowances toward the tan fabric. Place a tan 3½" square on the lower-right corner of each blue square, sew, trim, and press. Make 32 blue units. Repeat using the red 5" squares and the cream 3½" and 2" squares. For these units, press seam allowances toward the red fabric.

Make 32 of each.

3 Sew two red and two blue units together, pressing the seam allowances as indicated. Make 16 blocks.

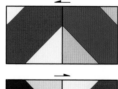

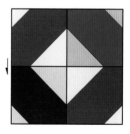

Make 16 of each.

Assembling the Quilt Top

1 Arrange the blocks into four rows of four blocks each. Sew the blocks into rows and sew the rows together, pressing the seam allowances as shown.

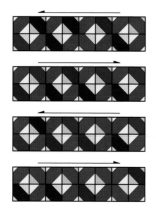

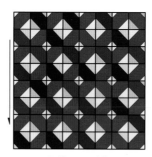

Quilt assembly

2 For the inner border, cut two of the red-print 2½"-wide strips to 36½" and sew them to the top and bottom of the quilt; press. Trim the remaining two strips to 40½"-long; sew them to the sides of the quilt and press.

3 For the outer border, sew together cream 5½"-wide strips as needed to cut two 40½"-long strips for the top and bottom borders and two 50½"-long strips for the side borders. The borders may be sewn to the quilt at this point, or you may choose to appliqué before attaching the borders. (If you appliqué first, be sure to leave the two large corner stars off and 5" of bias vine free at the corners until after the borders have been sewn to the quilt.)

4 Join the blue tone-on-tone 1½"-wide bias strips end to end and press the seam allowances open. Fold the bias strip in half *wrong sides* together and press lightly. Sew a scant ¼" from the raw edges.

Fold

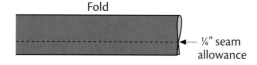

¼" seam allowance

5 Insert the bias bar into the bias tube make in step 4 and roll the seam allowance so it is centered along one flat side of the bias bar. Press the bias tube flat. Move the bias bar along the inside of the bar and press, continuing until the entire tube is flat. Remove the bias bar and press again. From this long strip, cut

four 5½"-long pieces for the short stems. Cut the remainder of the strip in half.

Bias bar

6 Position the bias vine and short stems first, referring to the photo on page 26 for approximate placement. Apply a few drops of appliqué glue to the wrong side of the vine and press it in place with your fingers, working your way down the border. Add the circles and stars next, and fuse in place. Machine appliqué using matching thread or monofilament.

Finishing the Quilt

For more information on finishing techniques, go to ShopMartingale.com/HowtoQuilt for free illustrated instructions.

1 Prepare the quilt backing.

2 Layer the quilt top, batting, and backing; baste the layers together.

3 Hand or machine quilt as desired.

4 Trim the backing and batting even with the quilt top, and then use the red-print 2"-wide strips to finish the edges of your quilt. Add a label and sleeve if desired.

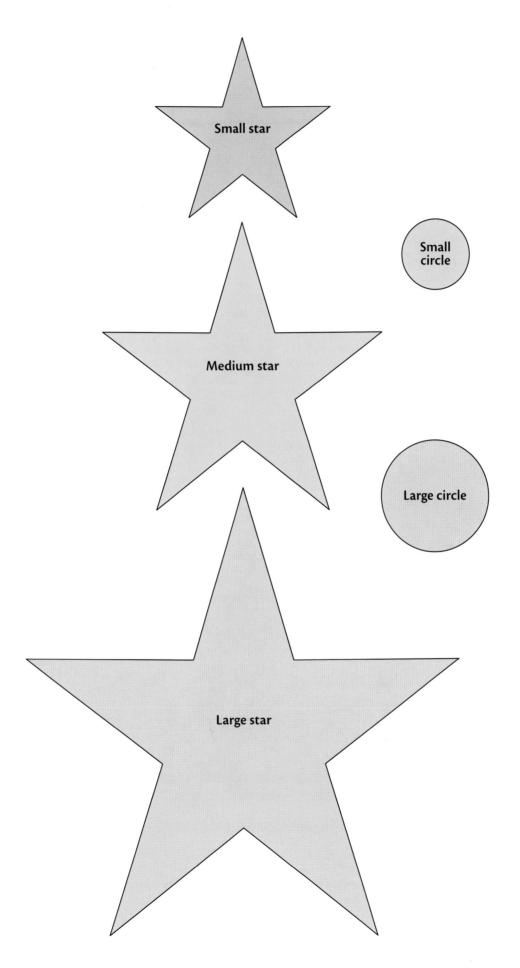

Small star

Small circle

Medium star

Large circle

Large star

Remember Me

Album blocks were quite popular in the 1800s. The light centers of the blocks were a place to gather signatures. In this scrappy version, the blocks interlock with splashes of red that form pinwheels.

Designed and made by Mary Etherington and Connie Tesene of Country Threads

Quilt size: 37½" x 47½" **Block Sizes:** Album: 7" x 7"; Pinwheel: 3" x 3"

Materials

Yardage is based on 42"-wide fabric.

1⅓ yards of muslin for blocks
1⅛ yards *total* of assorted dark scraps for blocks
⅝ yard *total* of assorted light scraps for blocks
½ yard *total* of assorted red scraps for Pinwheel blocks
⅜ yard of dark-blue print for binding
1⅝ yards of fabric for backing
41" x 51" piece of batting

Cutting

Measurements include ¼"-wide seam allowances.

Cutting for 1 Album Block
(Make 20.)
From *1* of the dark scraps, cut:
4 rectangles, 1½" x 3½"
8 squares, 1½" x 1½"

From the muslin, cut:
4 squares, 2½" x 2½"
8 squares, 1½" x 1½"

From *1* of the light scraps, cut:
1 rectangle, 1½" x 3½"
2 squares, 1½" x 1½"

Cutting for 1 Partial Block
(Make 12.)
From *1* of the dark scraps, cut:
4 rectangles, 1½" x 3½"
8 squares, 1½" x 1½"

From *1* of the light scraps, cut:
1 rectangle, 1½" x 3½"
2 squares, 1½" x 1½"

From the muslin, cut:
8 squares, 1½" x 1½"

Cutting for the Pinwheel Blocks
From the red scraps, cut:
62 squares, 2⅜" x 2⅜" in matching pairs; cut squares in half diagonally to yield 124 triangles

From the muslin, cut:
62 squares, 2⅜" x 2⅜"; cut squares in half diagonally to yield 124 triangles

Cutting for Background Rectangles
From the muslin, cut:
14 rectangles, 2½" x 3½"

Cutting for Binding
From the dark-blue print, cut:
5 strips, 2¼" x 42"

Making the Album Blocks

Use one light print, one dark print, and muslin for each block. Make 20 blocks total.

1 Sew a dark 1½" square between two muslin 1½" squares. Press the seam allowances toward the dark square. Sew a dark 1½" x 3½" rectangle to the unit. Press the seam allowances toward the rectangle. Make four side units.

Make 4.

2 Sew a light 1½" square between two dark 1½" squares. Press the seam allowances toward the dark squares. Make two units. Sew a light 1½" x 3½" rectangle between the two units just made. Press the seam allowances toward the pieced units. Make one center unit.

Make 1.

3 Join the four side units from step 1, the center unit from step 2, and four muslin 2½" squares. Press the seam allowances as indicated. The block should measure 7½" x 7½". Make 20 blocks.

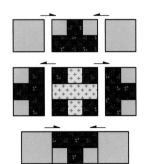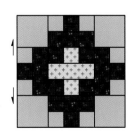

Albumn block.
Make 20.

Making the Partial Blocks

Use one light print, one dark print, and muslin for each partial block. Make 12 total.

1 Repeat steps 1 and 2 for the Album blocks; do not join the units yet.

Side units.
Make 4.

Center unit.
Make 1.

2 Join two side units and one center unit. Press the seam allowances toward the side units. Set aside the remaining two side units to be used when arranging the rows. Repeat to make 12 partial blocks.

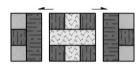

Partial block.
Make 12.

Making the Pinwheel Blocks

1 Join a red 2⅜" triangle with a muslin 2⅜" triangle. Press the seam allowances toward the red triangle. Make four matching units.

Make 4.

2 Join the four units from step 1. Press the seam allowances as indicated. The block should measure 3½" x 3½". Make 31 blocks.

Make 31.

Assembling the Quilt Top

1 Arrange the Album blocks, Pinwheel blocks, partial Album blocks, and muslin 2½" x 3½" rectangles in rows. Make sure to place matching segments of the partial Album blocks together. Sew the units between the Album blocks together before joining the row.

2 Sew the blocks and units together in rows. Press the seam allowances as indicated by the arrows. Join the rows. Press the seam allowances in one direction.

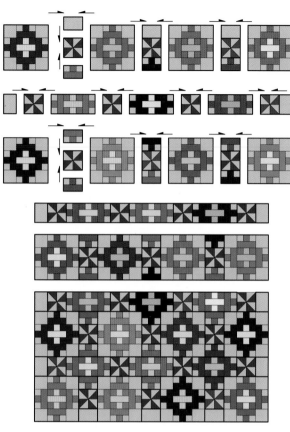
Quilt assembly

Finishing the Quilt

For more information on finishing techniques, go to ShopMartingale.com/HowtoQuilt for free illustrated instructions.

1 Prepare the quilt backing.

2 Layer the quilt top, batting, and backing; baste the layers together.

3 Hand or machine quilt as desired.

4 Trim the backing and batting even with the quilt top, and then use the dark-blue 2¼"-wide strips to bind your quilt. Add a label and sleeve if desired.